BOOK 4

the POINTER SYSTEM

for the
Piano

A Fast, Easy and Direct Approach to the Learning of Chords and Melodies on the Piano

HAL•LEONARD® CORPORATION

7777 W. BLUEMOUND RD. P.O. BOX 13819 MILWAUKEE, WI 53213

TABLE OF CONTENTS

SONGS

In your playing of three-four and four-four rhythm thus far, you have played the bass note having the same name as the chord (C Bass with the C Chord, F Bass with the F Chord, etc.).

To get more variety in the bass part it is possible to **"alternate"** the bass------that is, play different basses with the same chord.

Actually the bass tone may be any note of the chord; for example, a C Chord is made up of the tones C, E and G-----**any** one of these tones may be used as the bass note.

We will begin the playing of alternating bass with one of the more frequently used alternating bass patterns. In this pattern the bass note changes from the chord name to the note played by the little finger in the Pointer Position of that chord. In other words---when playing the C Chord, change or "alternate" the bass note from C to G; with the F Chord alternate from F to C; with the G7 Chord alternate from G to D, etc.

NOTE: The alternate bass is played an octave below the key played by the little finger in the Pointer Position. See the example to the right:

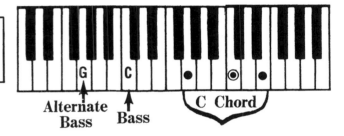

In three-four time alternate the bass when the same chord is used for more than one measure. Now play the section of melody below. The bass notes are indicated for you.

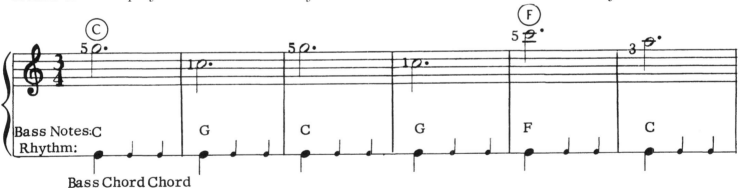

In four-four time alternate the bass when the same chord is used for more than two counts.

Now play the section of melody below. Again, the bass notes are indicated for you.

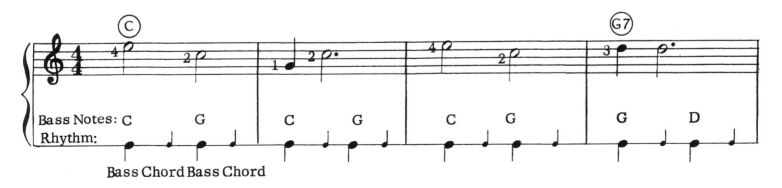

4

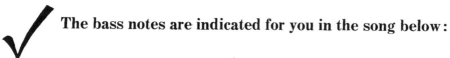

The bass notes are indicated for you in the song below:

CHORDS USED IN THIS SONG:

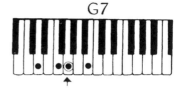

THE SIRENS WALTZ

Waldteufel

CHORDS USED IN THIS SONG:

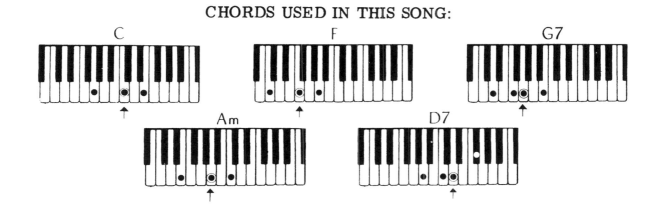

BICYCLE BUILT FOR TWO

Dacre

Here's a helpful hint to improve your sustaining pedal technique. When you are playing a song that moves along at a fairly fast tempo, depress the sustaining pedal on count 1 and release just as you strike the chord on count 2. Then depress the pedal again on count 3 and repeat the same procedure. The result will be a sharper sounding rhythm.

CHORDS USED IN THIS SONG:

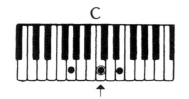
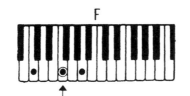
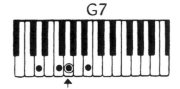

LITTLE BROWN JUG

Joe Winner

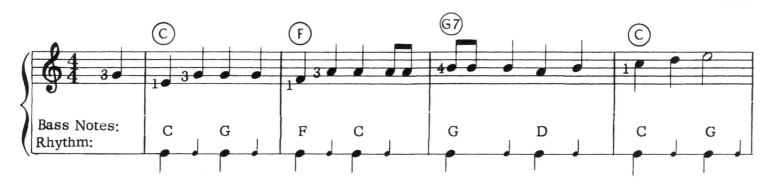

(continue rhythm)

Add the alternating bass to some of the songs you already know. **Remember**-----the alternate bass has the same letter name as the key played by the little finger in the Pointer Position of chords.

"Phrasing" is the punctuation in music, or how you "treat the notes". The two basic types of phrasing are legato and staccato.

Legato means that the notes are to be played smoothly and connected and is often indicated by a curved line (⌒) extended over a group of notes.

Staccato means that the notes are to be played in a disconnected manner and is indicated by a dot under or over the note (♪̣ ♪̇). To play staccato phrasing strike the key lightly and release immediately.

For practice in playing legato and staccato phrasing play the "Keyboard Pointers" below. **Do not use the sustaining pedal.**

A fuller sound can be achieved by playing the melody line "in octaves". An octave, you will remember, is the distance of eight keys from a particular letter name key, up or down, to a key of the same letter name; for example, from C up or down eight keys to another C.

Start playing the melody in octaves with the familiar song below. Play the melody note (large note) with your thumb and the octave note (small note) with your little finger.

Begin by practicing only the melody in octaves. Place your thumb and little finger on the first note, E, in the span of an octave----**and play the keys with a downward motion from the wrist.** To replay the same keys-----**lift the entire hand with an upward motion from the wrist and press the keys down again.** To move to different keys----**lift the entire hand from the keys, again with an upward motion from the wrist----and without changing the distance between the thumb and little finger, move the hand to the next note.**

Add the bass and chord accompaniment only after your hand has become accustomed to the octave span and you can change easily from one octave to the next.

> **NOTE:** To make your wrist more flexible and enable you to perfect this new playing technique faster, play the C Scale up and down the keyboard in octaves.

FOR HE'S A JOLLY GOOD FELLOW

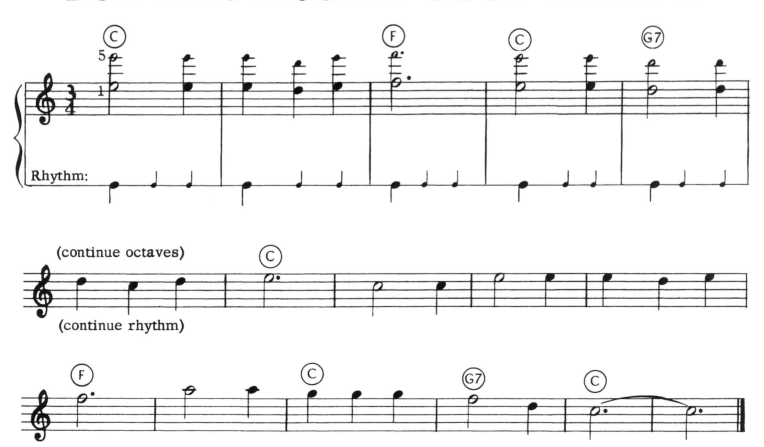

(continue octaves)

(continue rhythm)

CHORDS USED IN THIS SONG:

EMPEROR WALTZ

Johann Strauss

CHORDS USED IN THIS SONG:

LA SPAGNOLA

Di Chiara

 Play the octave style with some of the songs you have learned previously. Choose songs in which the melody line does not move large distances from one note to the next.

One sixteenth note is written like this:

Two or more sixteenth notes are written like this:

In Book 1 you learned that one count (or one quarter note) consists of a **downbeat** and an **upbeat.** You also studied diagrams showing the splitting of one beat into halves (or two eighth notes).

To play sixteenth notes we will split the beat again; **one count** is then divided into **four equal parts** (or four sixteenth notes). Thus each sixteenth note gets one-fourth beat.

To the right is a diagram illustrating the splitting of one count into first, two notes; then, four notes. Notice the counting.

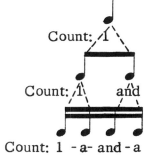

Count: 1

Count: 1   and

Count: 1 - a- and - a

For practice in playing sixteenth notes play the exercise below. The counting is indicated for you. Notice also the $\frac{2}{4}$ time signature. There are two counts in each measure.

CHORDS USED IN THIS SONG:

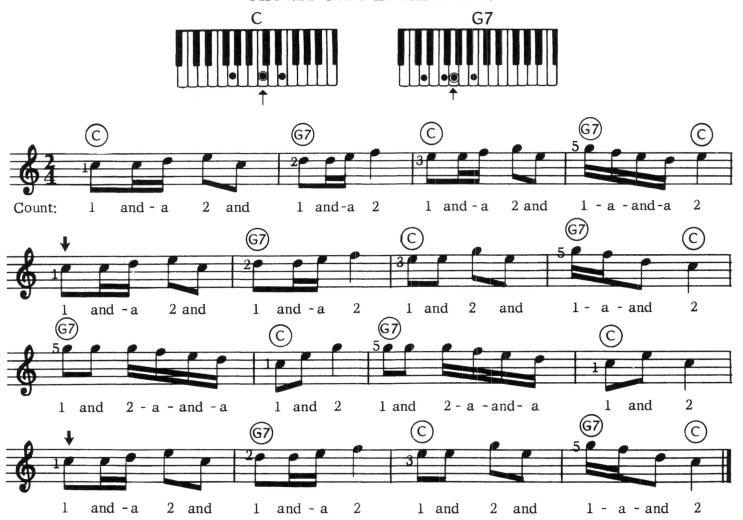

The dotted eighth followed by a sixteenth ( ) is a rhythm pattern that you will find often in music. The two notes combined get one count. The diagrams below show how the count is divided and how to play this pattern with a left hand rhythm accompaniment.

Three sixteenths and one dotted eighth have the same time value ---3/4 count.

(See measure 1)

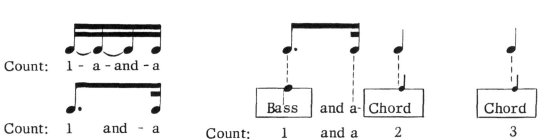

Count: 1 - a - and - a

Count: 1 and - a

Count: 1   and a   2   3

CHORDS USED IN THIS SONG:

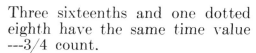

LOVE'S OLD SWEET SONG

Molloy

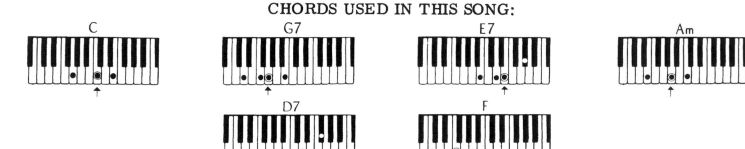

(continue rhythm)

Practice this "Keyboard Pointer" with both legato and staccato phrasing. Do not use the sustaining pedal.

See the examples below:

LEGATO ⟶

STACCATO ⟶

To avoid the use of ledger lines above the staff and to facilitate reading of the melody line an [8va] indication will be used for some of the songs that follow.

8va-----means to play the melody line an **octave** or **eight notes higher than written.**

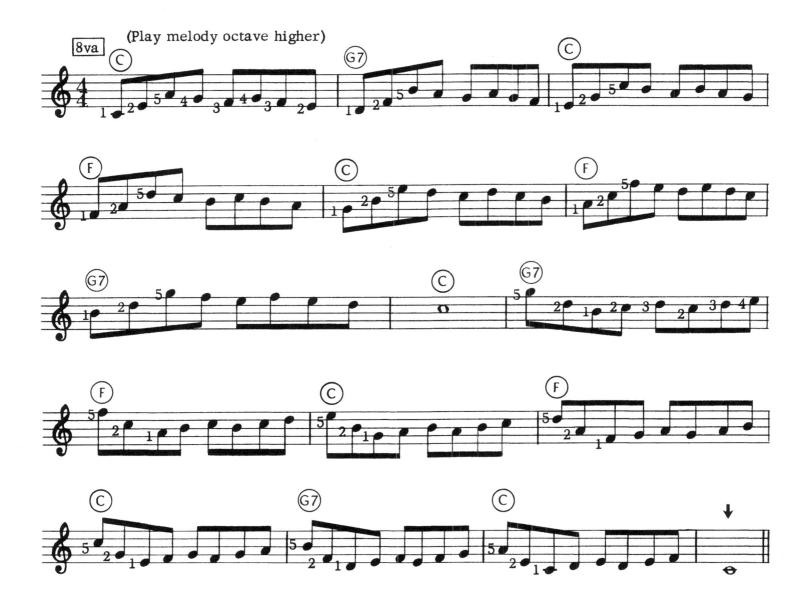

(Play melody octave higher)

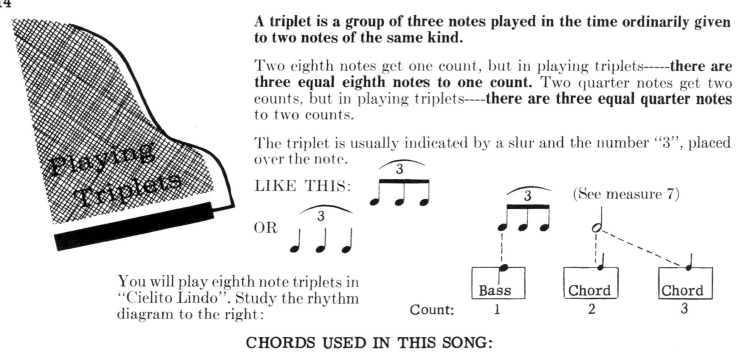

A triplet is a group of three notes played in the time ordinarily given to two notes of the same kind.

Two eighth notes get one count, but in playing triplets-----**there are three equal eighth notes to one count.** Two quarter notes get two counts, but in playing triplets----**there are three equal quarter notes** to two counts.

The triplet is usually indicated by a slur and the number "3", placed over the note.

LIKE THIS:

OR

You will play eighth note triplets in "Cielito Lindo". Study the rhythm diagram to the right:

(See measure 7)

| Bass | Chord | Chord |
| Count: 1 | 2 | 3 |

CHORDS USED IN THIS SONG:

CIELITO LINDO

Fernandez

Play Bb in this song.

Rhythm:

(continue rhythm)

In the song below you will play both the dotted eighth and sixteenth and the triplet rhythm patterns.

CHORDS USED IN THIS SONG:

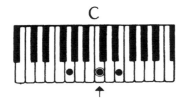 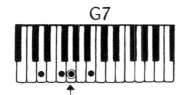 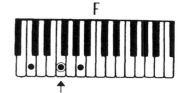

JUANITA

Norton

16

In this course you have played songs with time signatures of $\frac{3}{4}$, $\frac{4}{4}$, or $\frac{2}{4}$. In each case the bottom number or "4" indicated that the quarter note received one count.

In $\frac{6}{8}$ time the top number indicates that there are **six** counts in each measure and the bottom number or "8" indicates that the **eighth note receives one count.** The quarter note will then get two counts.

Play the song below, counting aloud. The counting is indicated for you. **Remember-----**each note will get twice as much time value as it received in four-four, three-four or two-four time.

CHORDS USED IN THIS SONG:

THE KERRY DANCE

CHORDS USED IN THIS SONG:

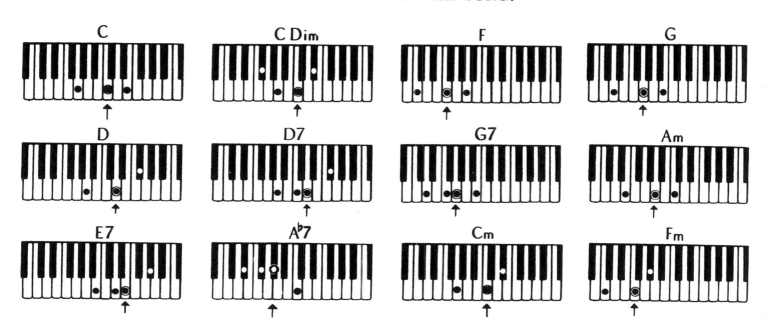

SWEET AND LOW

Barnby

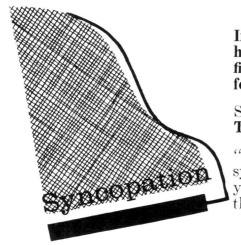

In playing rhythm you have found that certain beats of the measure have a strong pulse or accent. Ordinarily the strong beats are on the first count in three-four time and the first and third counts in four-four time.

Sometimes the accent is shifted from a strong beat to a weak beat. **This is called "syncopation".**

"Hello My Baby" is an example of syncopation. Notice that the syncopated notes have been marked with an accent sign (>). As you play the melody, strike the accented notes harder. Before you add the rhythm study the rhythm patterns below.

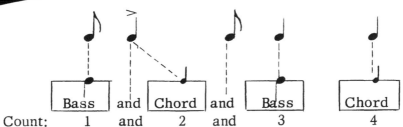

HELLO MY BABY

Howard

Here is another melody in which you will find syncopation. The syncopated notes are again accented for you. Study the rhythm patterns below. This song is written in 2/4 time.

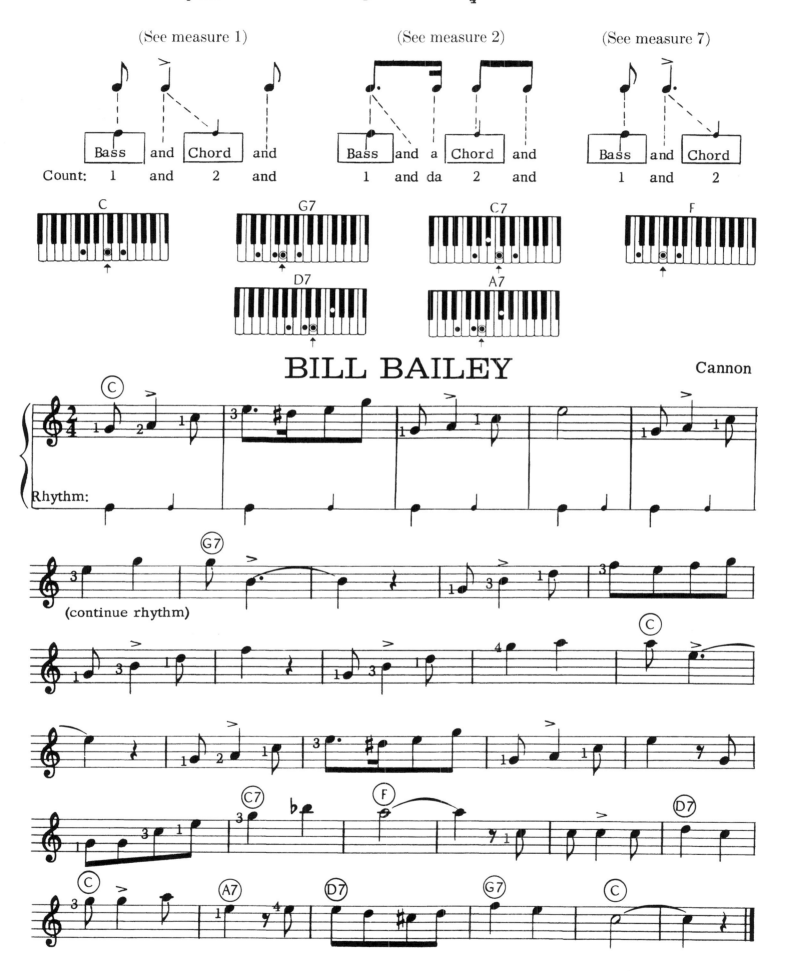

Here is a "Keyboard Pointer" in which you will use several different keyboard techniques. Do not use the sustaining pedal.

1. **Rhythm**-----play a rhythm in three; count aloud as you play.

2. **Phrasing**-----watch for the **legato** and **staccato** markings; also, play the correct fingering.

3. **Double notes**-----notice that you will play double notes in the right hand part; strike both notes at the same time.

Have you noticed in your playing thus far that certain chord sequences appear more frequently than others? Examples in the Key of C Major are the changes from C to G7 and C to F.

The diagrams below illustrate a different way of changing from the C Pointer Chord to the G7 or F Chord. These changes represent your first study of different positions of chords. As you progress, you will learn different positions of all chords.

TO GO FROM C TO G7:

1. Play the C Pointer Chord.
2. Place the middle finger on the key below the Pointer finger.
3. Raise the Pointer finger and thumb to the next white key above.
4. The little finger remains on the same note for both chords.

THE NEW G7 CHORD ⟶

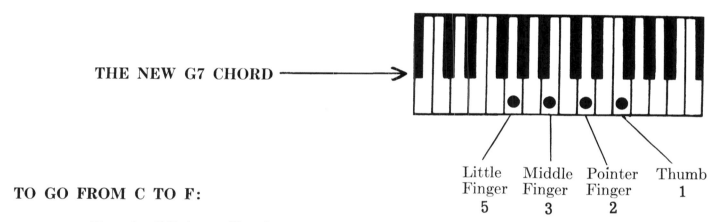

TO GO FROM C TO F:

1. Play the C Pointer Chord.
2. Raise the thumb to the next white key above.
3. With the ring finger play the next white key above the key played by the little finger in the C Pointer Chord.
4. The Pointer finger remains on the same key for both chords.

THE NEW F CHORD ⟶

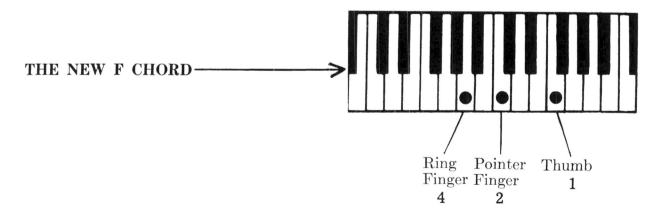

 As you play the new G7 and F Chord positions in the next song, you will notice that your hand moves only a short distance on the keyboard as you change from one chord to the next.

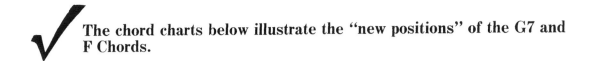

The chord charts below illustrate the "new positions" of the G7 and F Chords.

CHORDS USED IN THIS SONG:
(Showing shortcut positions)

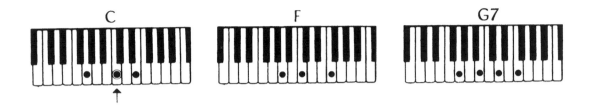

OLD FOLKS AT HOME

Foster

(Play melody octave higher)

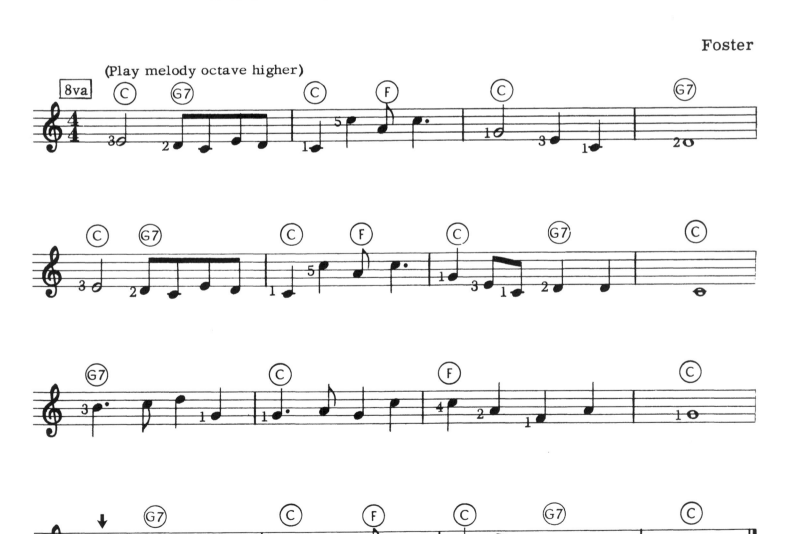

CHORDS USED IN THIS SONG:
(Showing shortcut positions)

C
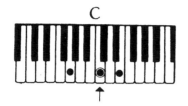

G7
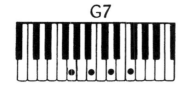

F
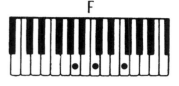

AMERICA

Henry Carey

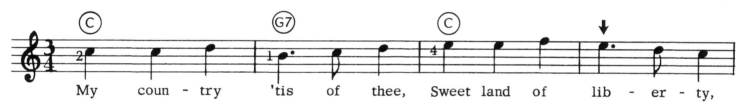

My coun - try 'tis of thee, Sweet land of lib - er - ty,

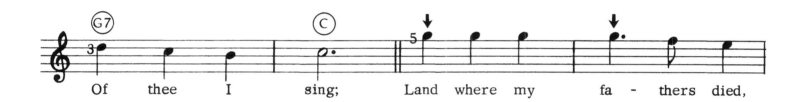

Of thee I sing; Land where my fa - thers died,

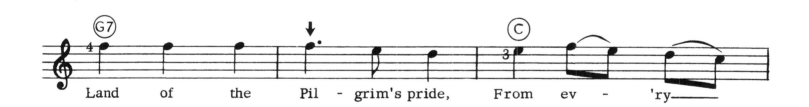

Land of the Pil - grim's pride, From ev - 'ry___

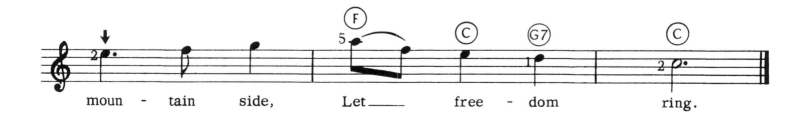

moun - tain side, Let___ free - dom ring.

...inuing to use the "chord shortcut", play the song below.   Notice that you will still play the D7 Chord in the Pointer Position **because this position affords the least possible movement in changing from one chord to the next.**

CHORDS USED IN THIS SONG:
(Showing shortcut positions)

MY BONNIE

Traditional

CHORDS USED IN THIS SONG:
(Showing shortcut positions)

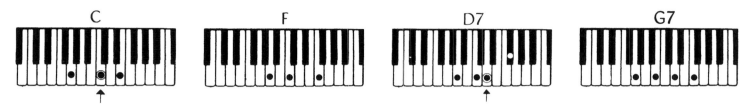

MY SWEETHEART'S THE MAN IN THE MOON

Thornton

My Sweet - heart's The Man In The Moon,_____ I'm

go - ing to mar - ry him soon,_____ 'Twould

fill me with bliss, Just to give him one kiss, But I

know that a doz - en I nev - er would miss, I'll go

up in a great big bal - loon,_____ And see my sweet -

heart in the moon,_____ Then be - hind some dark cloud, where no -

one is al - lowed, I'll make love to the man in the moon._____

Using the new chord positions play a rhythm accompaniment with the next two songs. Employ fingerings for the chords that seem to be the most natural hand position for you. For example, although you finger the new F Chord 4-3-1 when playing sustained chords, it is probably easier to play it 5-3-1 when playing rhythm.

CHORDS USED IN THIS SONG:
(Showing shortcut positions)

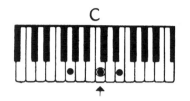 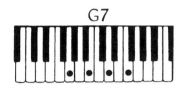 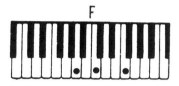

BEAUTIFUL BROWN EYES

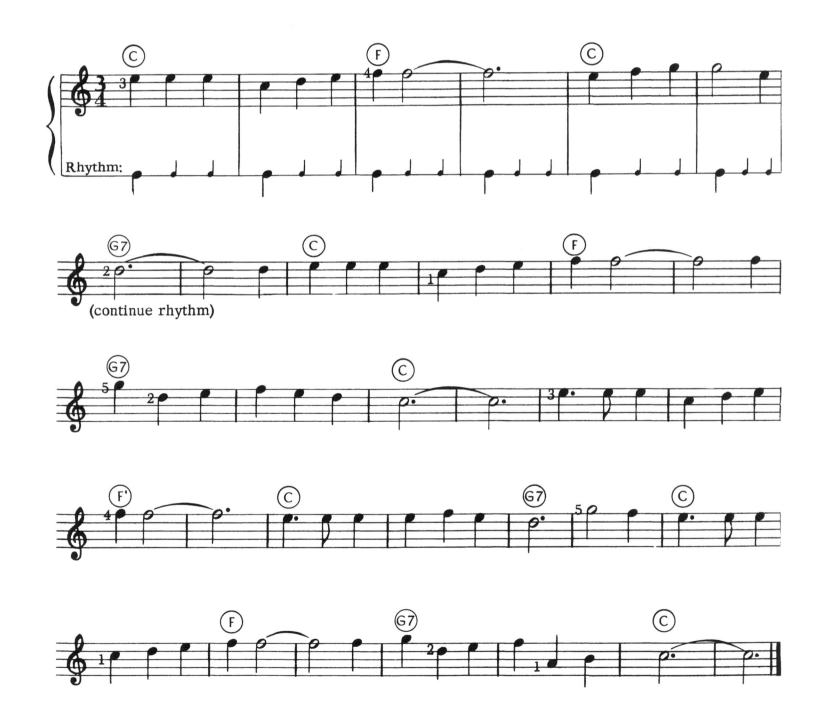

CHORDS USED IN THIS SONG:
(Showing shortcut positions)

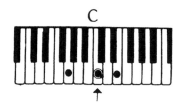 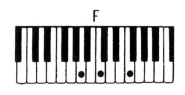 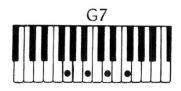 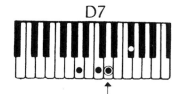

SAILING, SAILING

Godfrey Marks

(continue rhythm)

Here are some interesting new left hand rhythm patterns in three-four and four-four time. Instead of playing the straight afterbeat rhythm, you will vary the bass and chord patterns.

The rhythm patterns are indicated in the same manner as previously used except that there is a rhythm line included for each staff. Again, the regular size note with the stem down (♩) indicates the **bass** and the smaller note with the stem up (♪) indicates the **chord.**

To play the new patterns-----decide first whether a note is a bass or chord; then, interpret the correct time value of each. For example, in the first measure of "Tres Jolie", the bass is played on count 1; the chord is played on count 2 and being a half note, is sustained for two counts.

CHORDS USED IN THIS SONG:

TRES JOLIE

Waldeufel

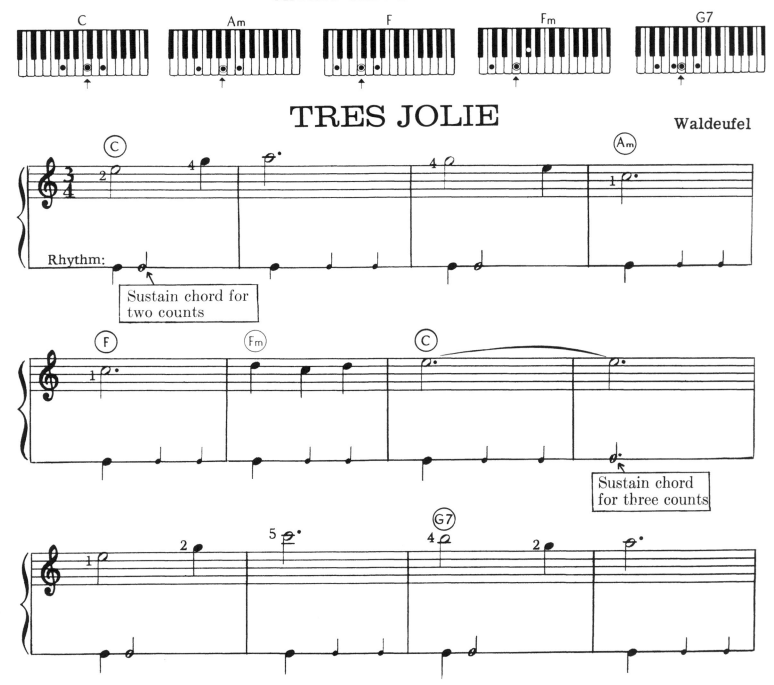

CHORDS USED IN THIS SONG:

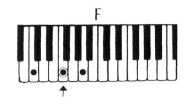 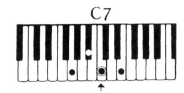 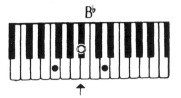

CIRIBIRIBIN

Pestalozza

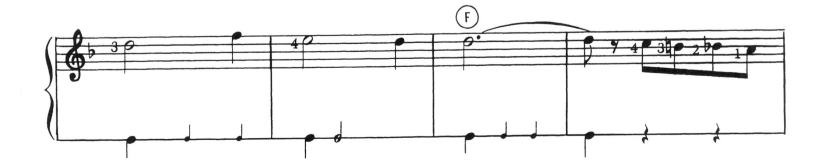

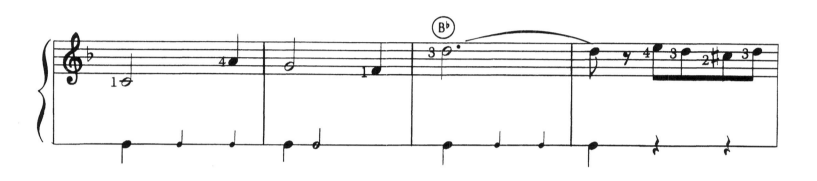

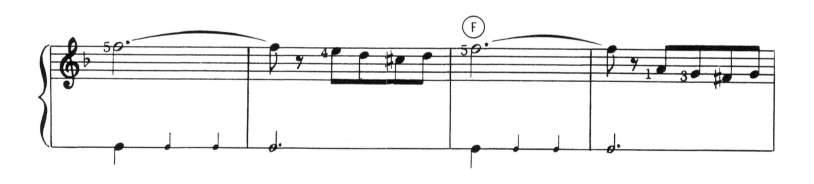

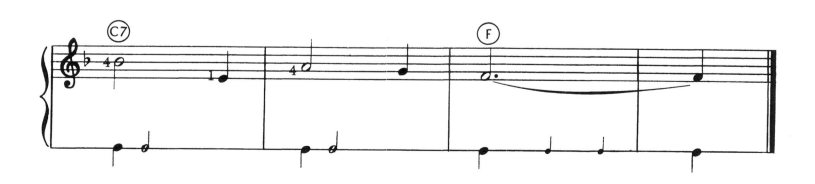

CHORDS USED IN THIS SONG:

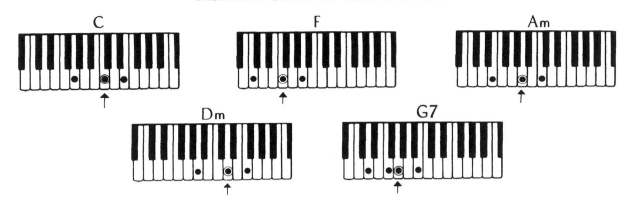

LOCH LOMOND

Traditional

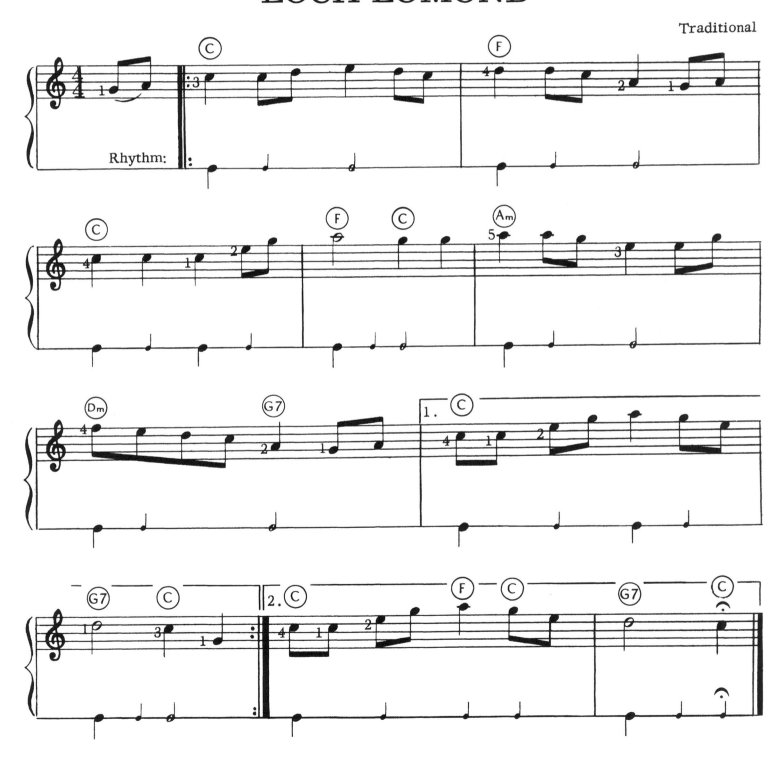